GOD LOVES MY FAMILY

ACTIVITY BOOK

By Carolyn Owens
Illustrated by Susan Morris

Unless otherwise stated, Scripture taken from THE HOLY BIBLE: NEW INTERNATIONAL VERSION®. Copyright © 1973, 1978, 1984 by International Bible Society. Used by permission of Zondervan Publishing House. All rights reserved.

The "NIV" and "New International Version" trademarks are registered in the United States Patent and Trademark Office by International Bible Society. Use of either trademark requires the permission of International Bible Society.

Copyright © 1995 Concordia Publishing House
3558 S. Jefferson Avenue, St. Louis, MO 63118-3968
Manufactured in the United States of America

Teachers may reproduce pages for classroom use only. Parents may copy pages when necessary for the completion of an activity.

All rights reserved. Except as noted above, no part of this publication may be reproduced, stored in a retrieval system, or transmitted, in any form or by any means, electronic, mechanical, photocopying, recording, or otherwise, without the prior written permission of Concordia Publishing House.

2 3 4 5 6 7 8 9 10 11   07 06 05 04 03 02 01 00 99 98

"JESUS LOVES"

Jesus loves you very much. Draw or glue your picture or a shiny piece of aluminum foil in the frame.

Jesus loves us so much, He gave His life on the cross to pay for our sins and rose again to win us eternal life in heaven. Write a thank-You prayer to Jesus in the heart.

Because Jesus died and rose again for you, you get to live with Him in heaven forever. Draw a line through the maze. Jesus is the Way!

God sent His Son, Jesus, to earth as a baby at Christmastime. He chose Joseph to be Jesus' earthly father. Jesus' mother was Mary. Fill out Jesus' birth certificate.

Joseph and Mary gave Jesus a loving home in Nazareth. On the bench, draw a toy that carpenter Joseph might have made for Jesus.

If baby food in jars had been available back in Bible times, what kinds of food do you think Mary would have given Jesus? Decorate the labels to show what's inside.

Do you think Jesus helped Joseph make some furniture for their house? Draw something Joseph and Jesus might have made.

Mary loved Jesus and took good care of Him. Decorate this blanket Mary might have sewn to keep Jesus warm.

God loves everyone in the world and wants all people to believe in Jesus as their Savior. Write the jobs of these people God loves. Then draw your picture. God loves you!

Find and color the pictures in this stained-glass window that help you see God's love for you.

God gave Jesus an earthly father and mother to love Him. God gives you a loving family too. Draw a picture of your home.

God loves you and your mom and dad, and your grandmas and grandpas, and your aunts and uncles and cousins. Do you need to tell some of these people about Jesus? Ask Him to help you. Then draw all the people in your family looking out of these windows.

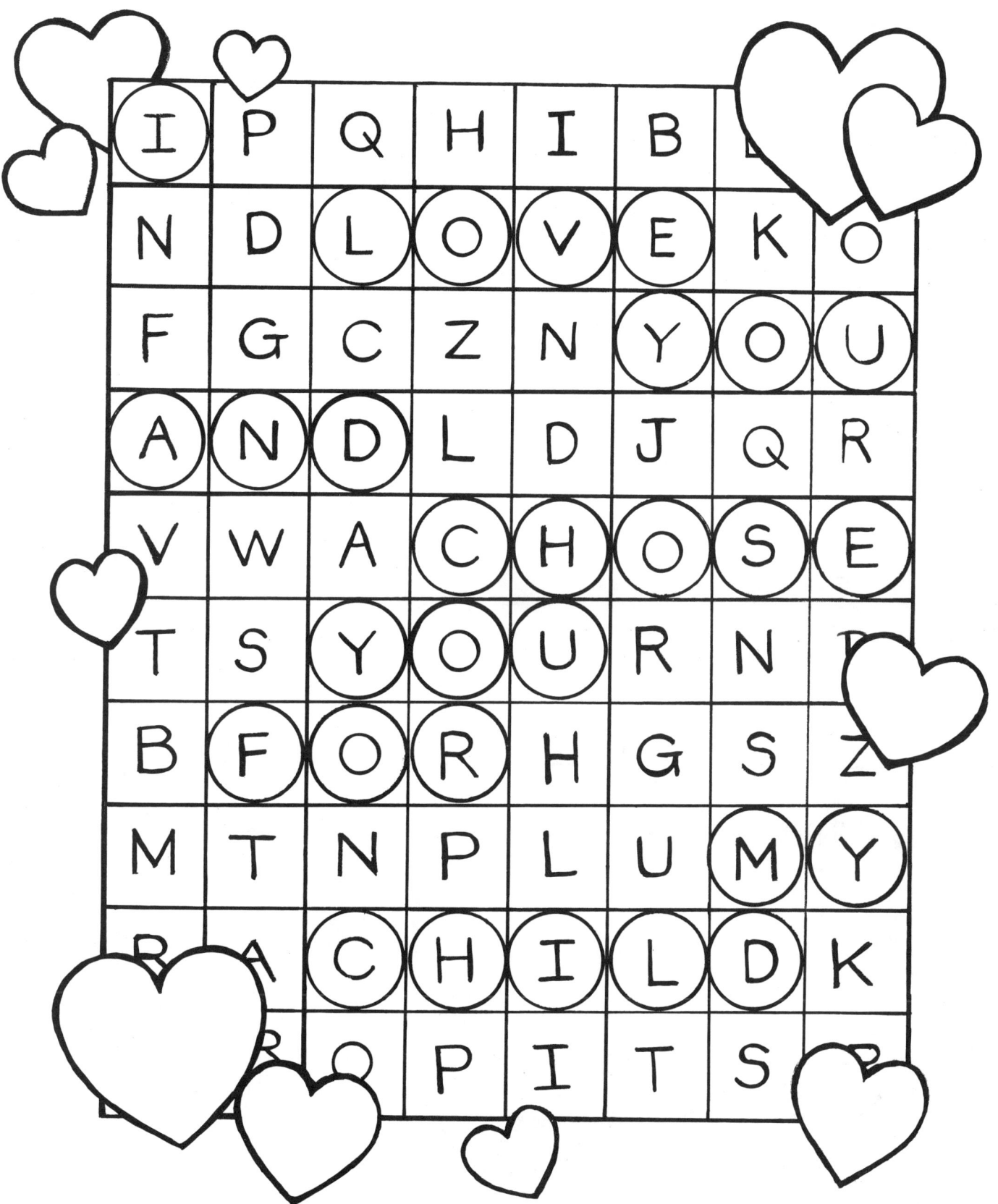

All people who know Jesus as their Savior are in God's family. God adopted you into His family when you were baptized. Color the circles to find God's secret message to you.

Sometimes a mother is not able to care for her baby or young child. When that happens, God can help a loving family adopt the child. Decorate a welcome card for a child who is being adopted by a new family.

God works through specially trained people to find homes for babies and children who need loving care. Draw lines to match these baby bears with the parents who will adopt them.

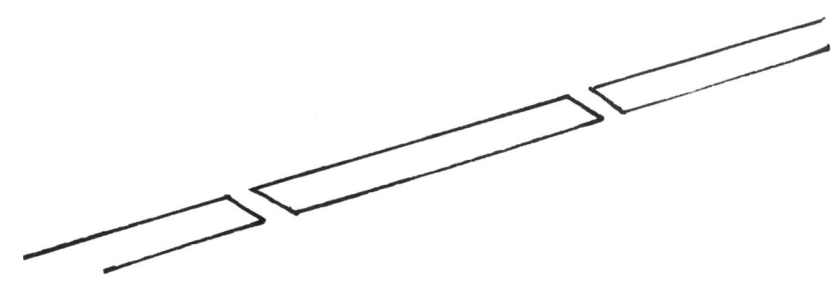

Whether you were born into your family or adopted, your parents were very happy to bring you home. Draw a car for this mom and dad so they can take their baby home.

18

The best thing your family does is to teach you about Jesus. Draw a line through this maze to help the parents tell their child about Jesus' love.

Circle and color the things you think a new mom and dad will buy for their baby.

Have you had a new baby at your house? That is a very happy time. Decorate this sign to welcome a new baby.

Because Jesus loved you enough to live and die for you, God adopted you into His family. Have you ever adopted a doll or stuffed animal or pet who needed a lot of love? Draw its picture here.

The new baby's grandmas and aunts have been busy sewing presents for it. Decorate the baby's bib they made.

It is an exciting time when a family picks a name for a new baby. Write down some good names for a girl baby and a boy baby.

What kind of present could you give a baby to help it start learning about Jesus' love? Draw the gift in the box.

You might have to help your mom carry a diaper bag for a new baby. Decorate this bag for a new baby.

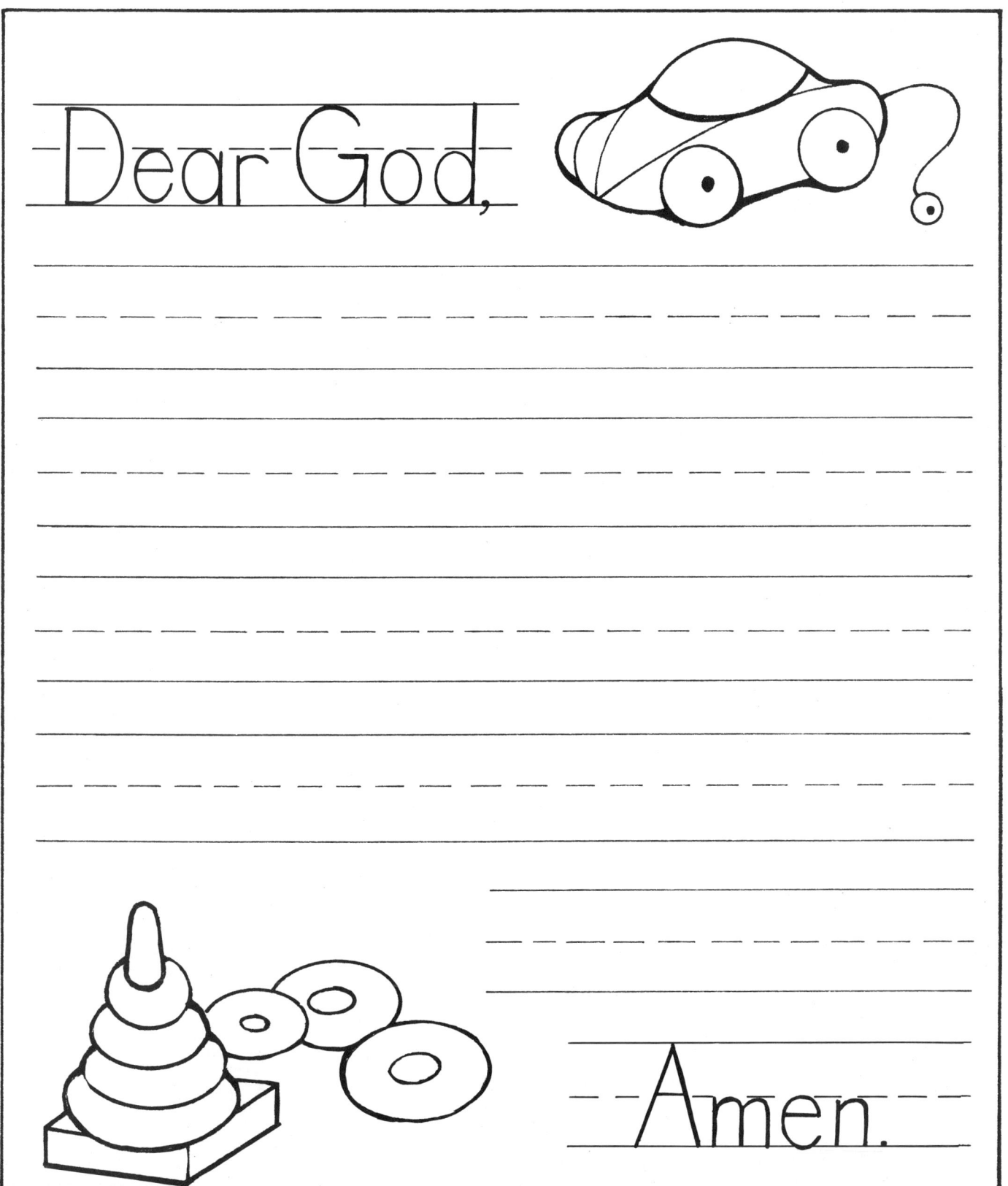

Some children live with a mom and a dad, some with a single parent. Some children live with their grandparents or other people who care for them. Write a letter to God thanking Him for the special people who love you.

When you go to bed at night, aren't you glad to have a grownup to help you say your prayers and tuck you in all snug? And God sends His angels to keep you safe all night. Draw your happy face inside this picture frame.

God loves you and your family. He teaches you about His love when you come to church and read His Word. He gives your family happy times together. Draw a picture of your family doing something fun together.

God loves you and your family and helps you keep Him first in your lives. Decorate the plaque to share God's love with your family.

Our heavenly Father is glad that you belong to Him. Draw pictures of how you looked when you were a baby and how you look now. Write in the date when you became God's child.

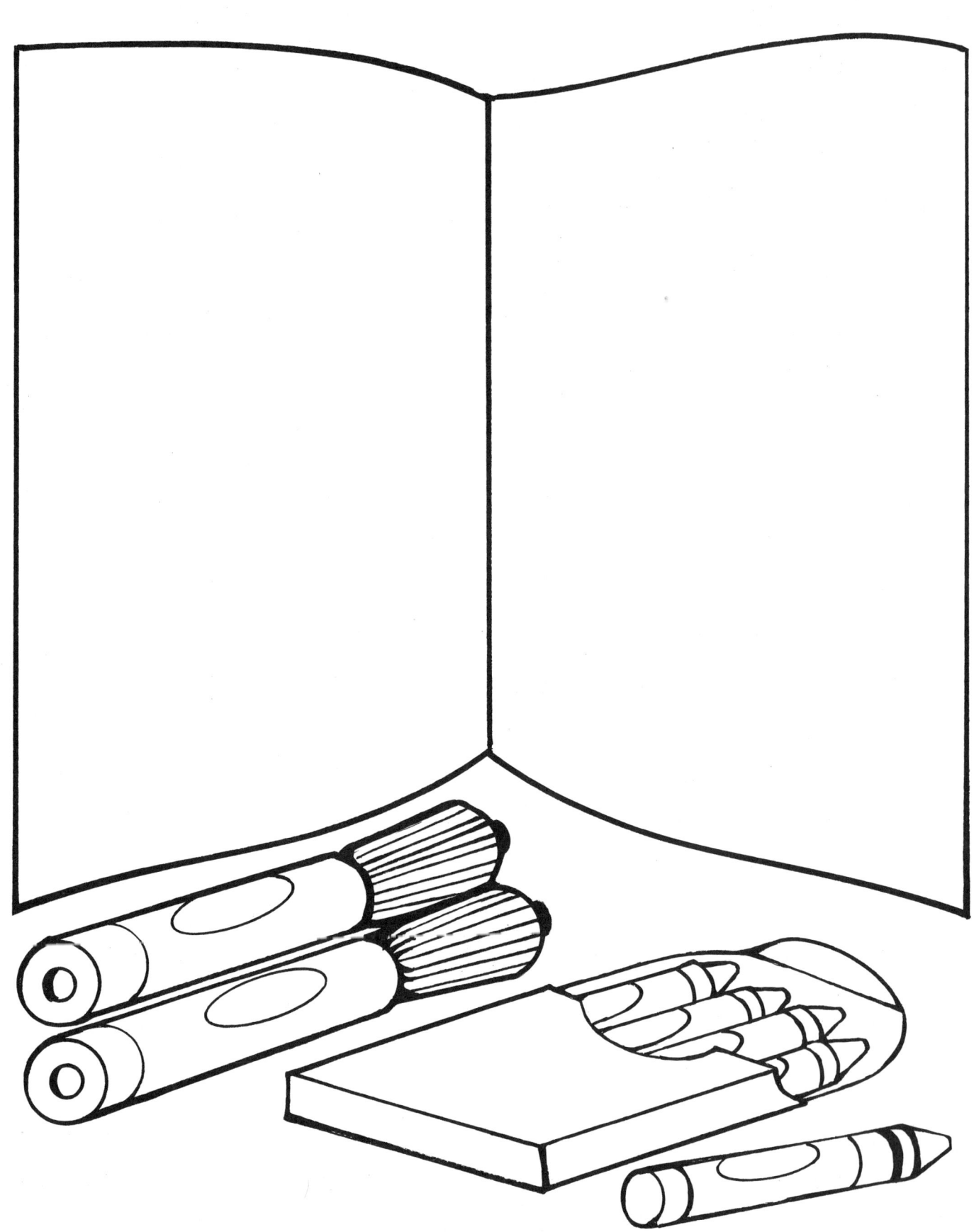

Does someone in your family live far away from you? Design a card for that person. Be sure and share Jesus' love.